Do not cut out
white space
between
arm and body.

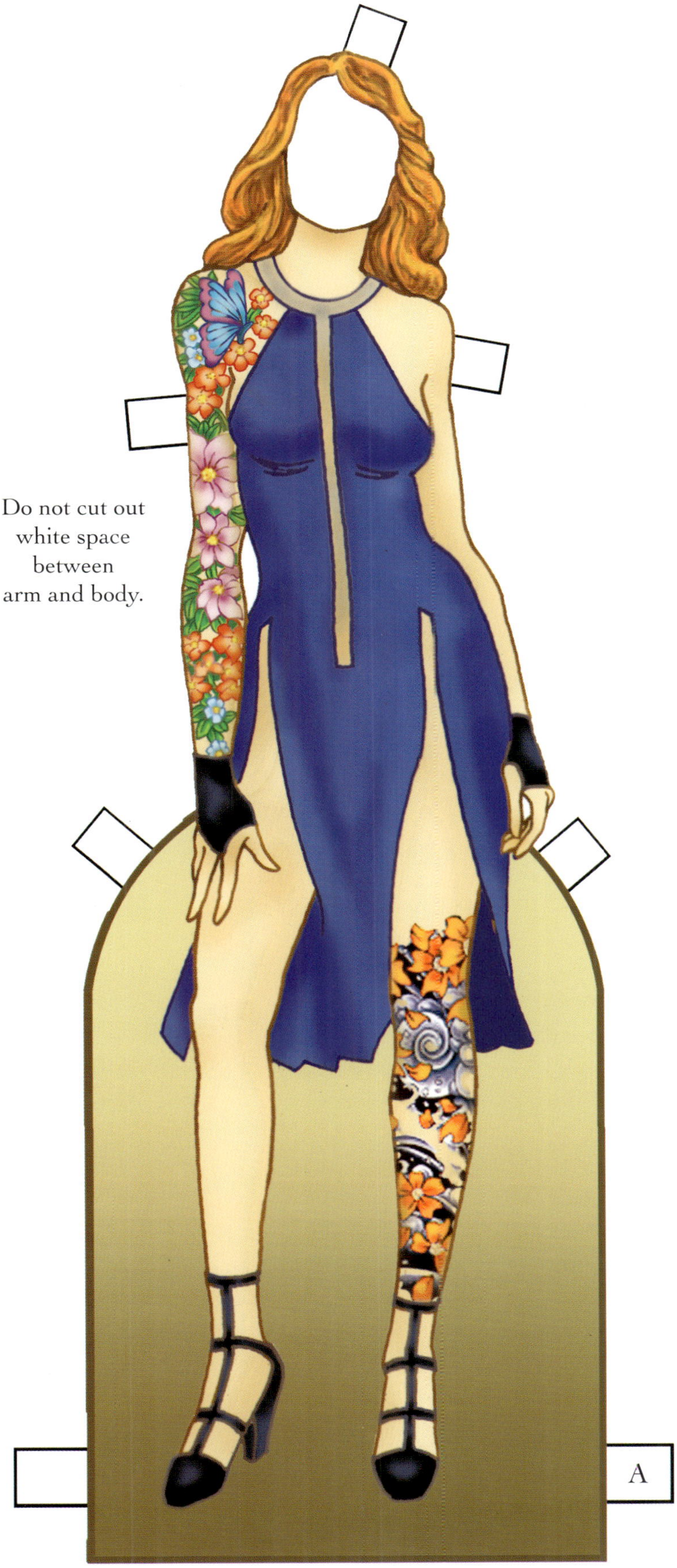

A

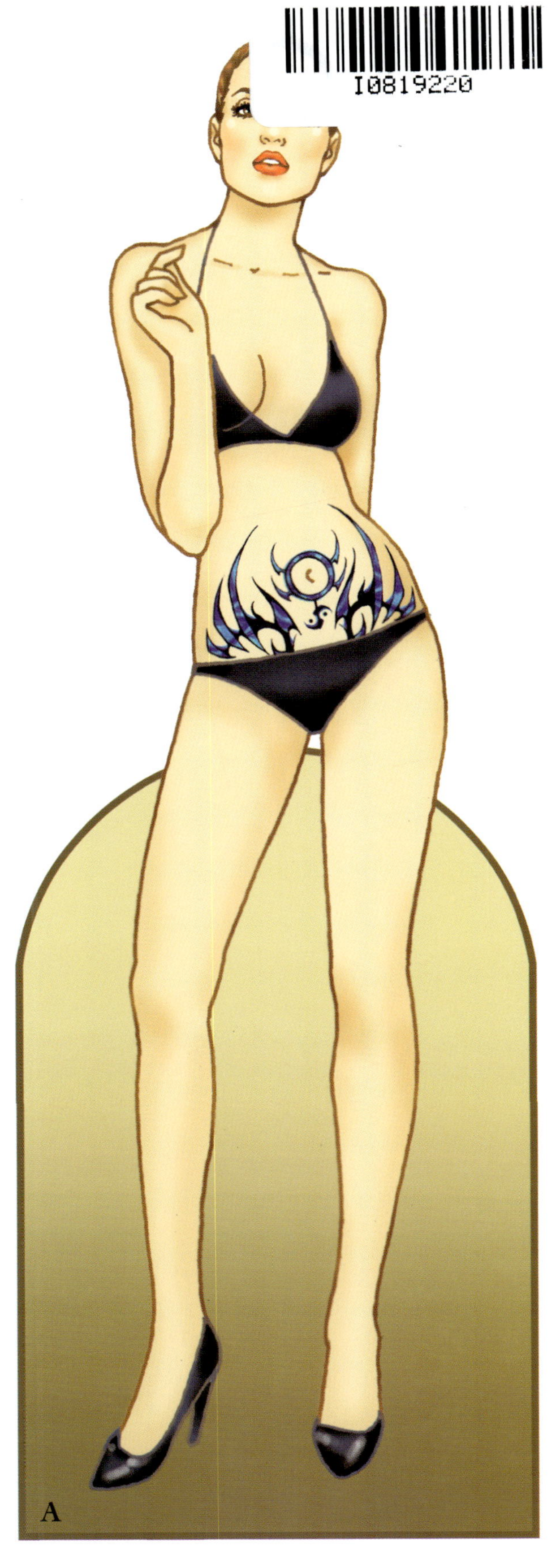

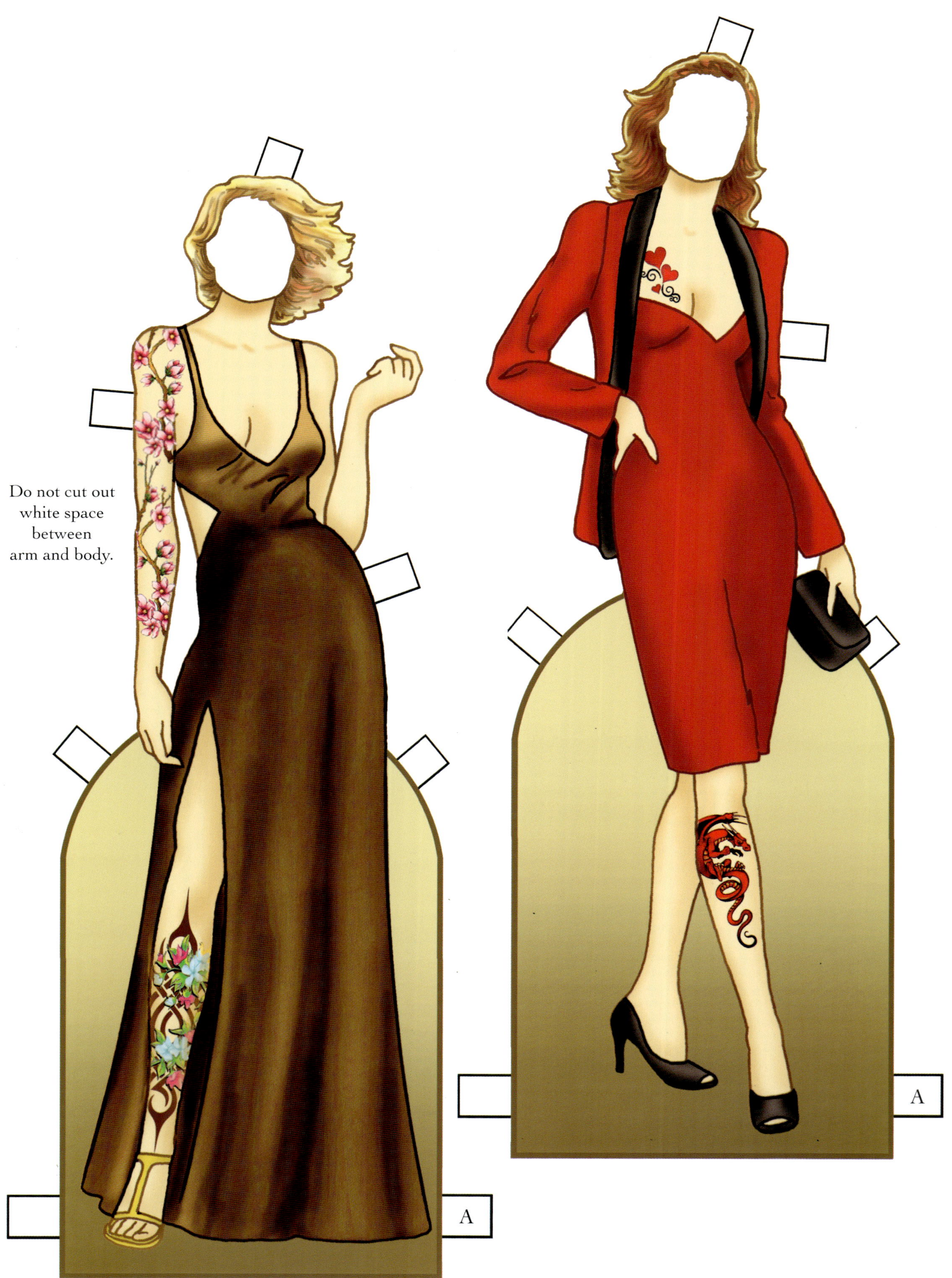
Do not cut out white space between arm and body.
A
A

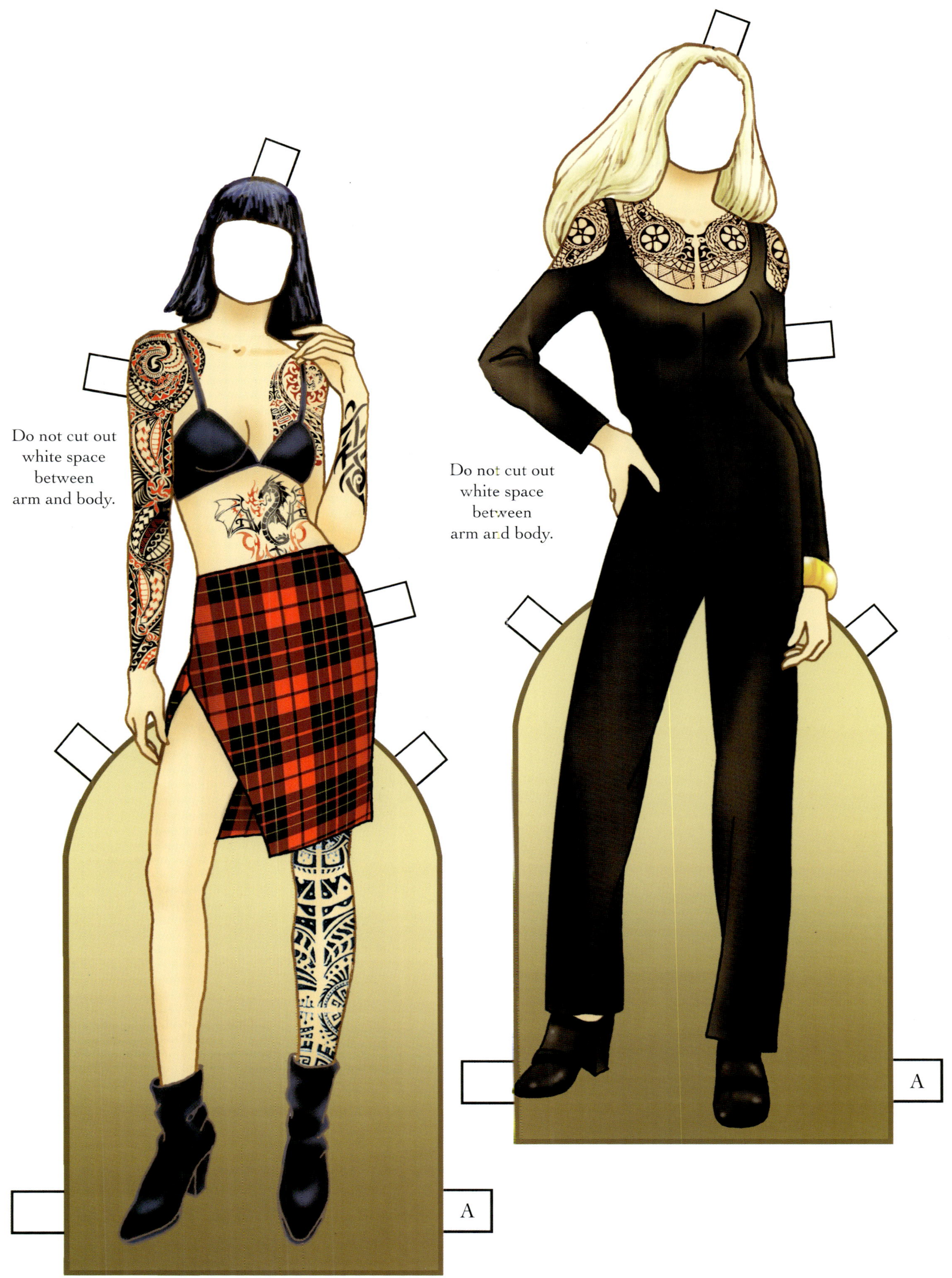
Do not cut out
white space
between
arm and body.
Do not cut out
white space
between
arm and body.
A
A

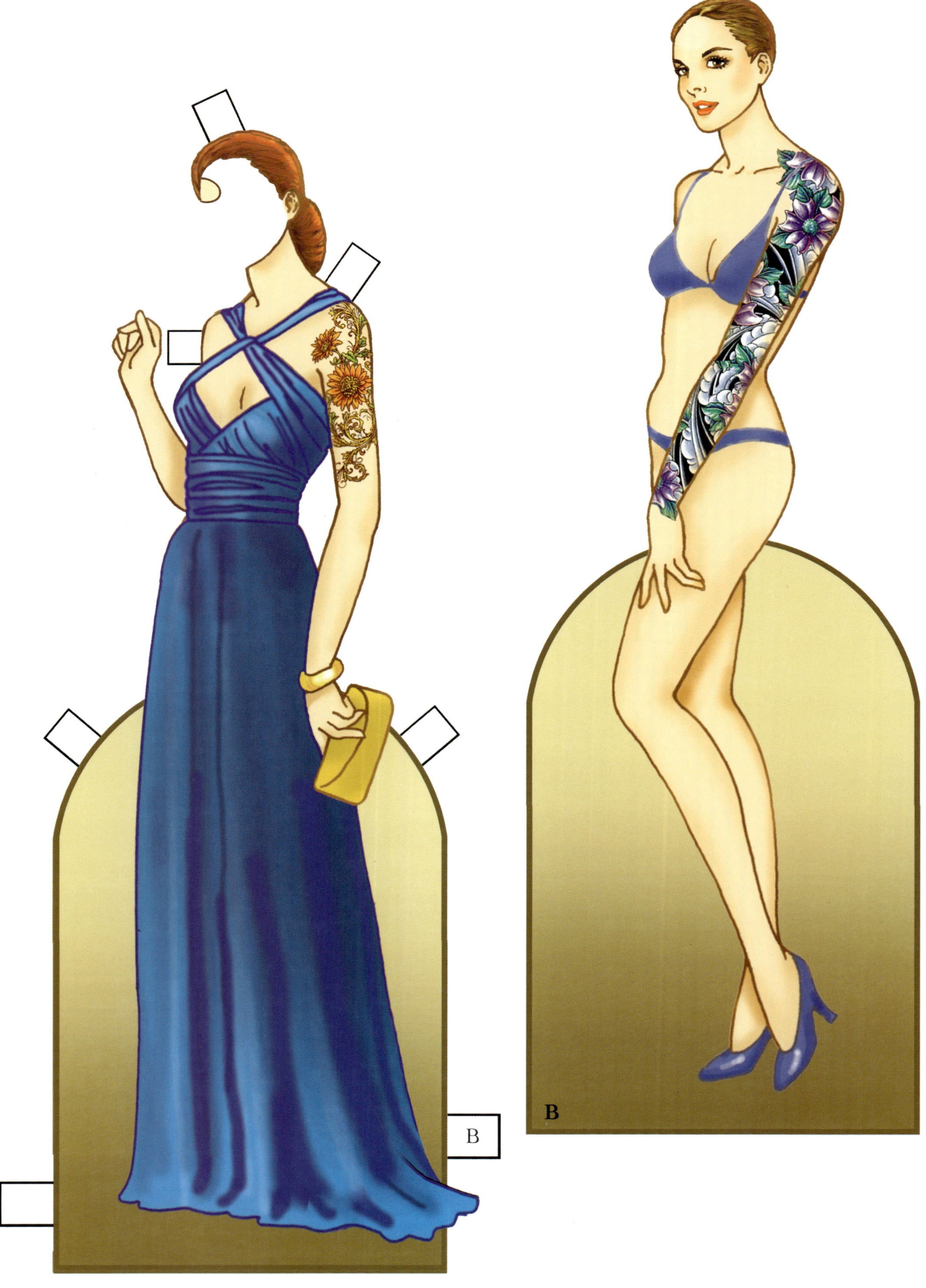
B
B

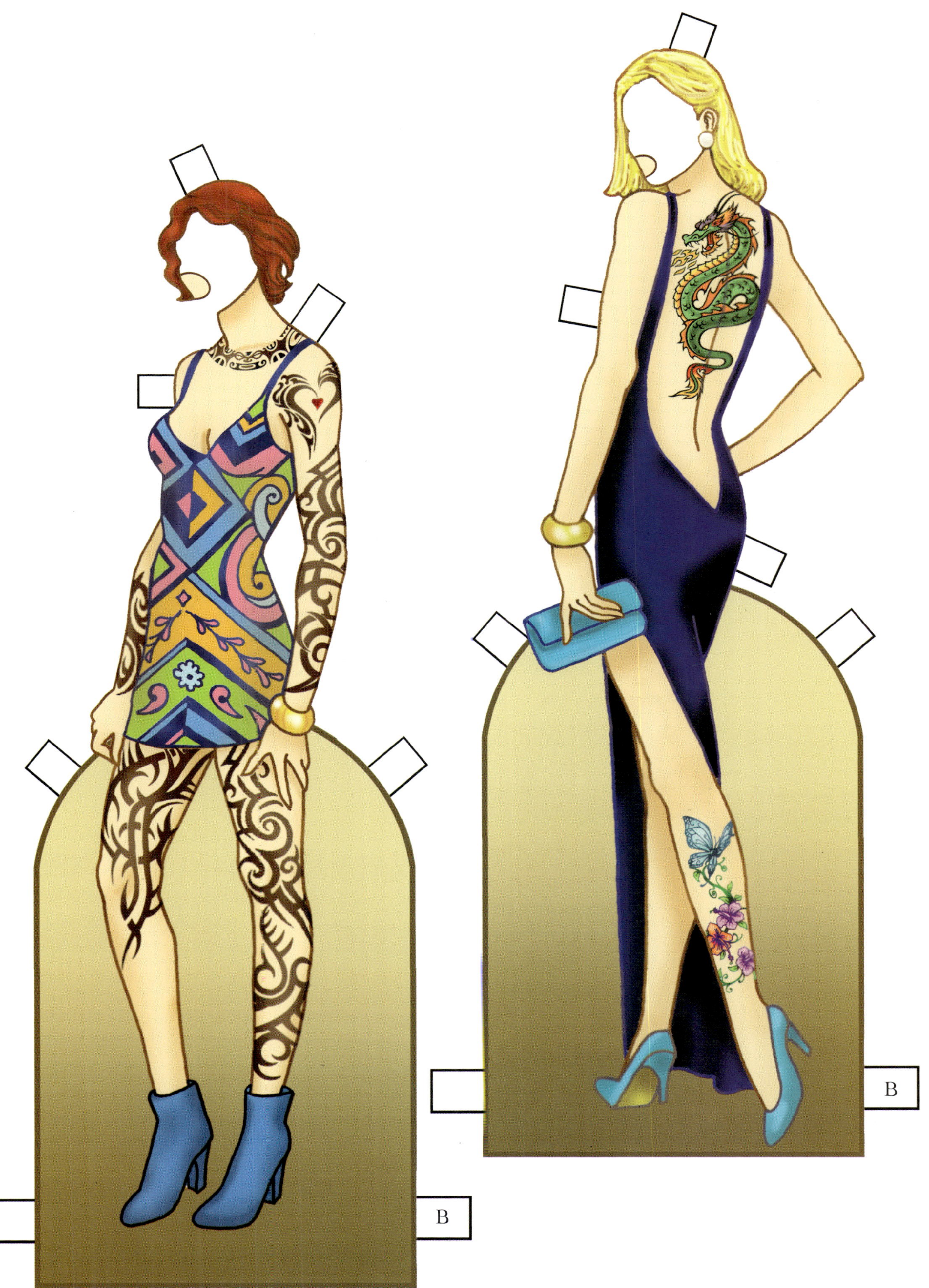
B
B

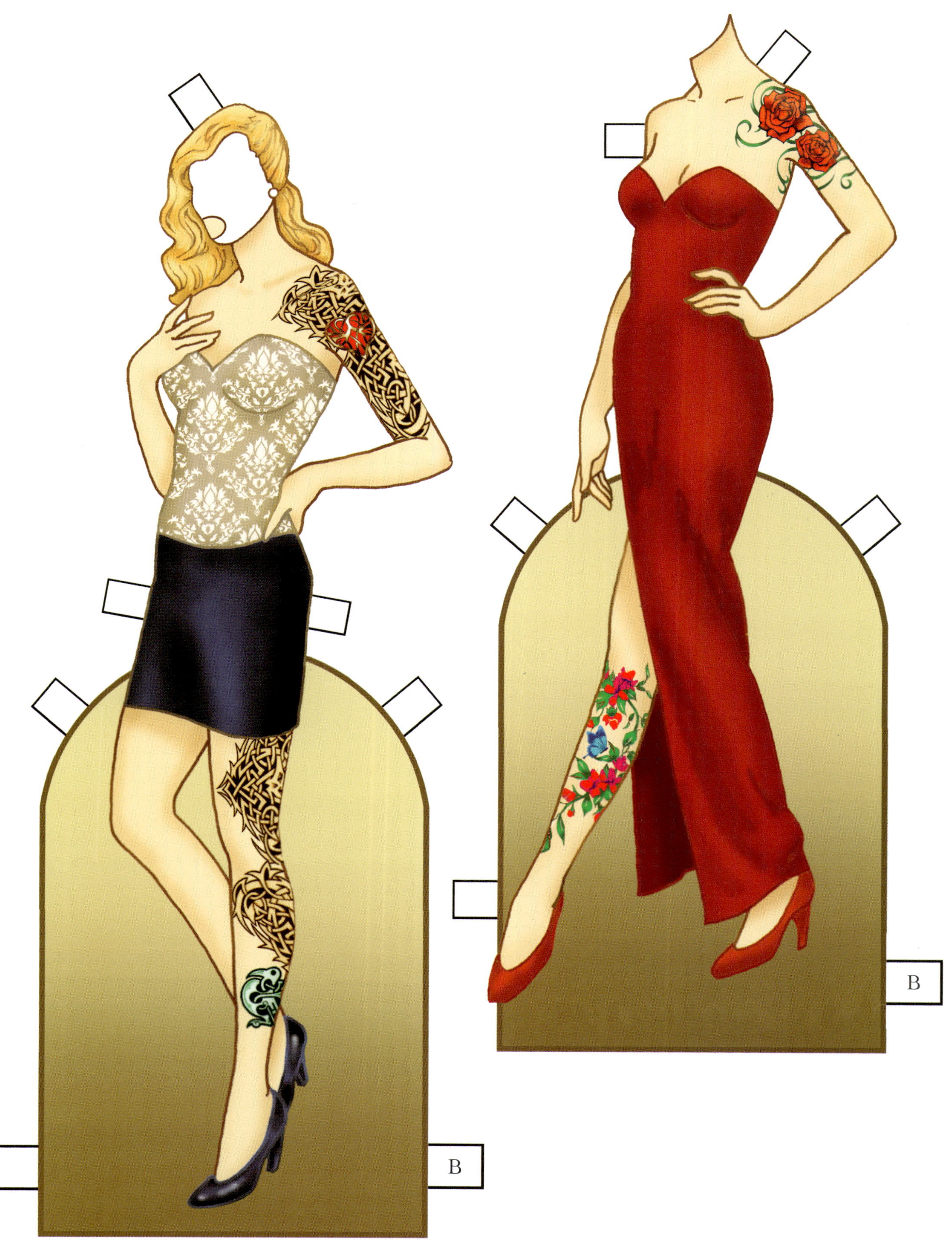
B
B

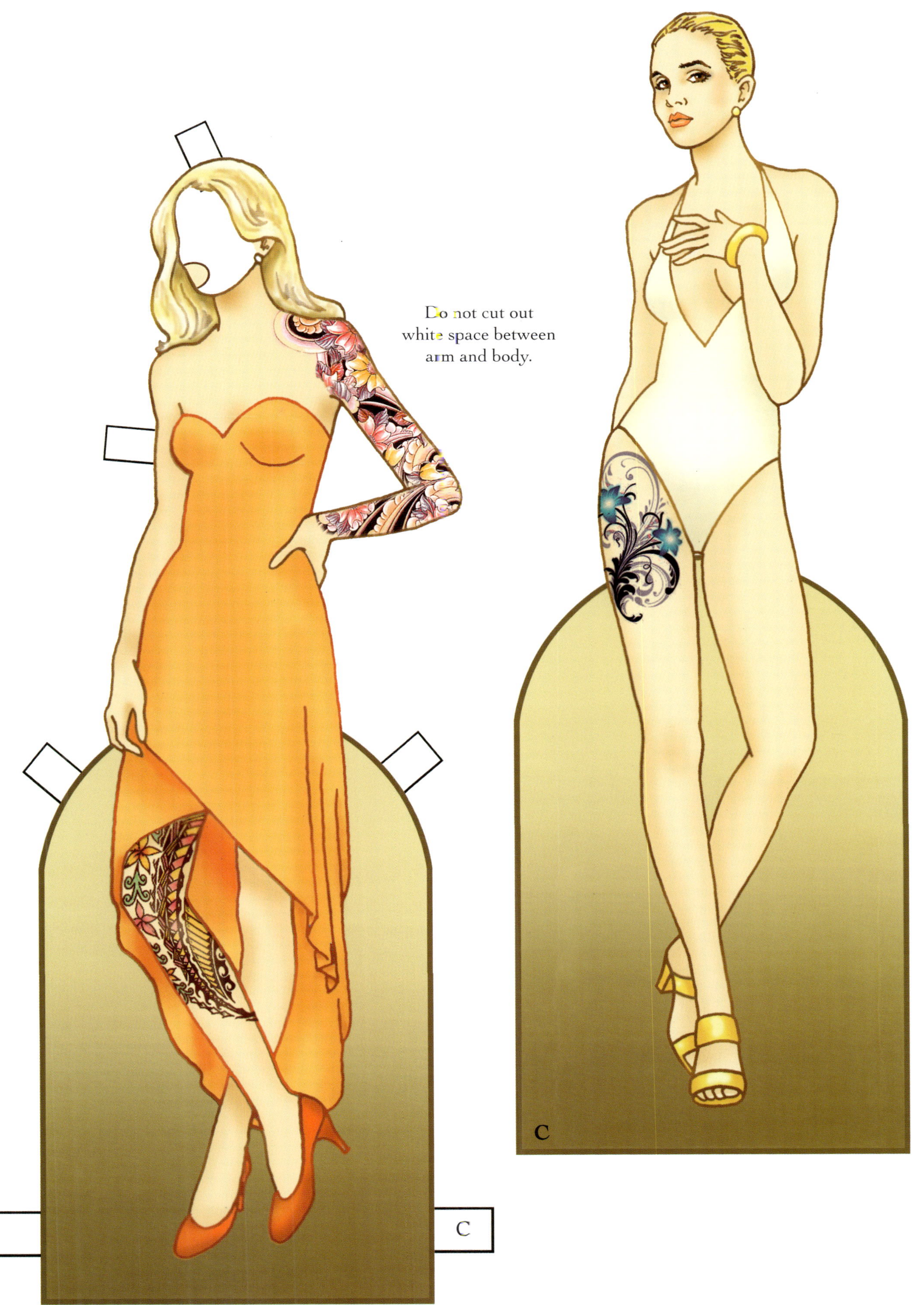
Do not cut out
white space between
arm and body.
C
C

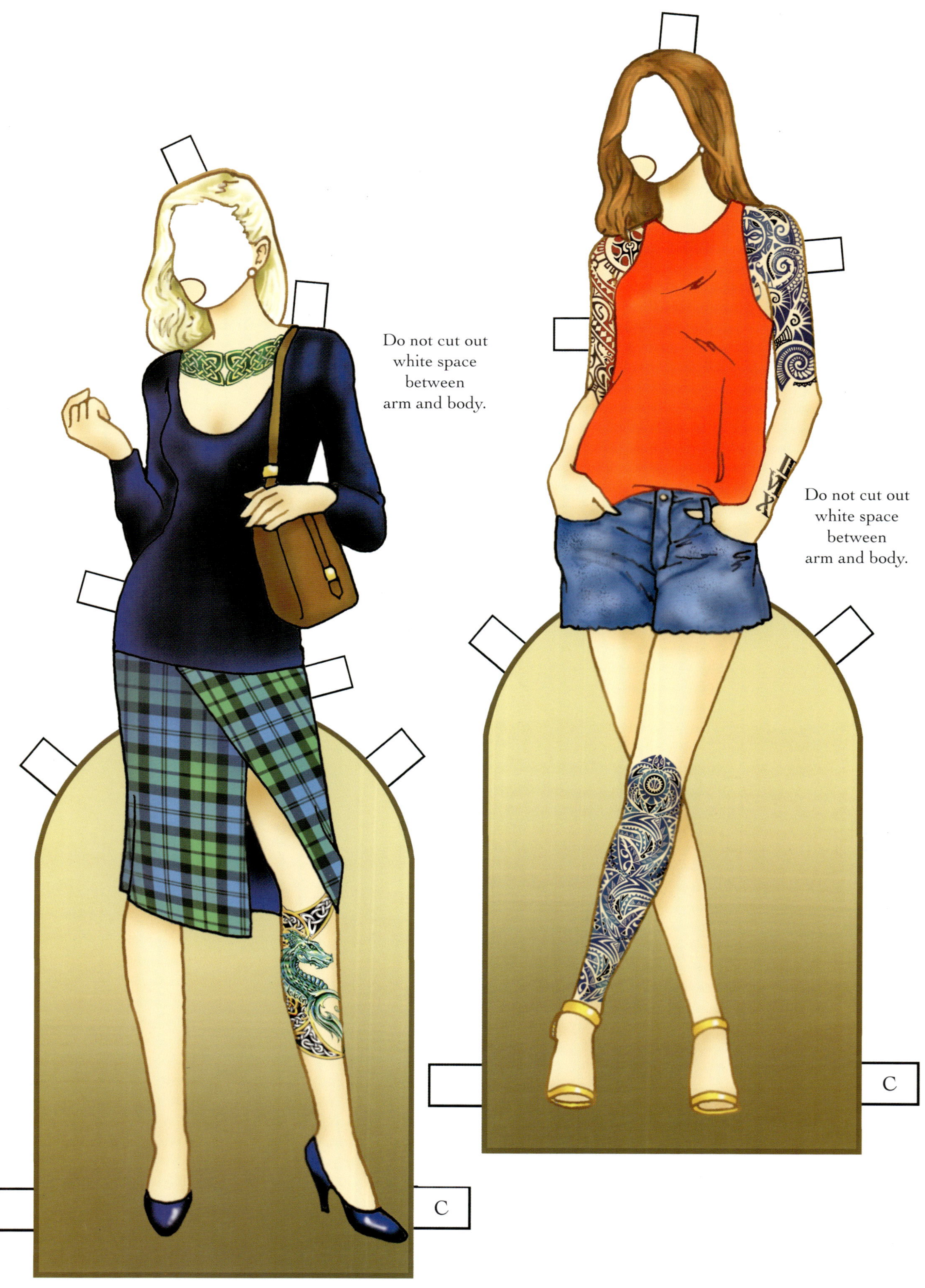
Do not cut out
white space
between
arm and body.
C
Do not cut out
white space
between
arm and body.
C

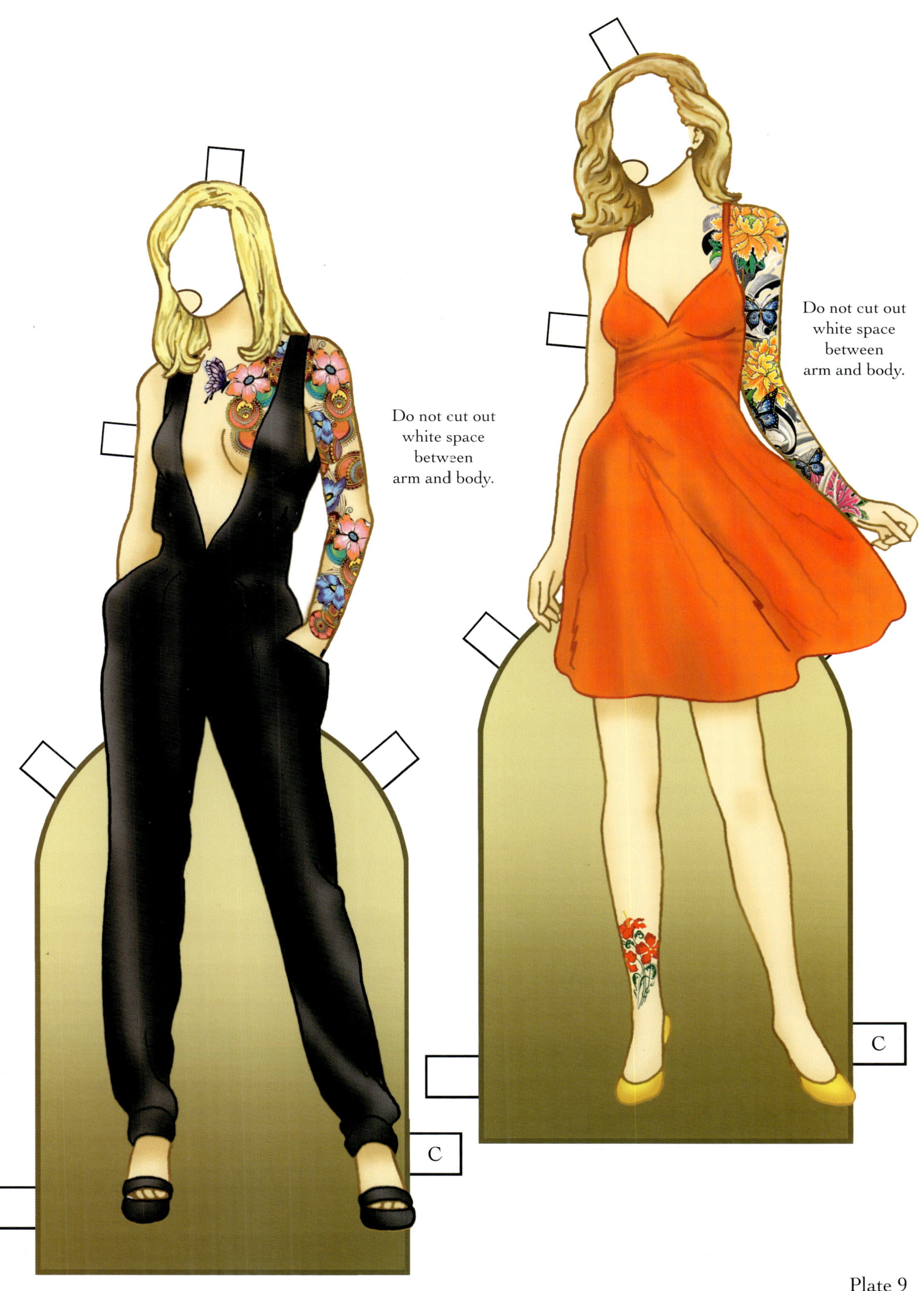
Do not cut out
white space
between
arm and body.
C
Do not cut out
white space
between
arm and body.
C

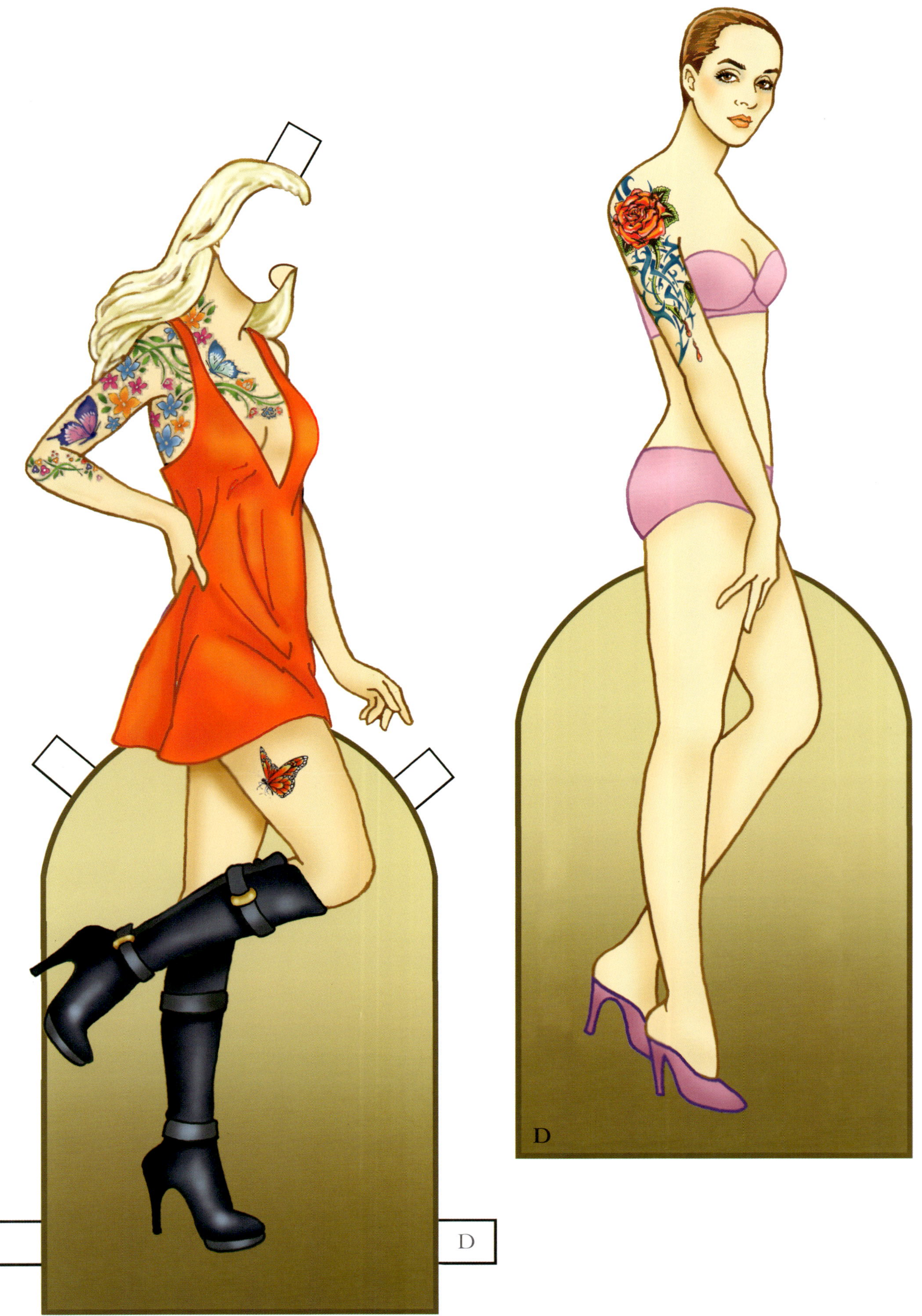
D
D

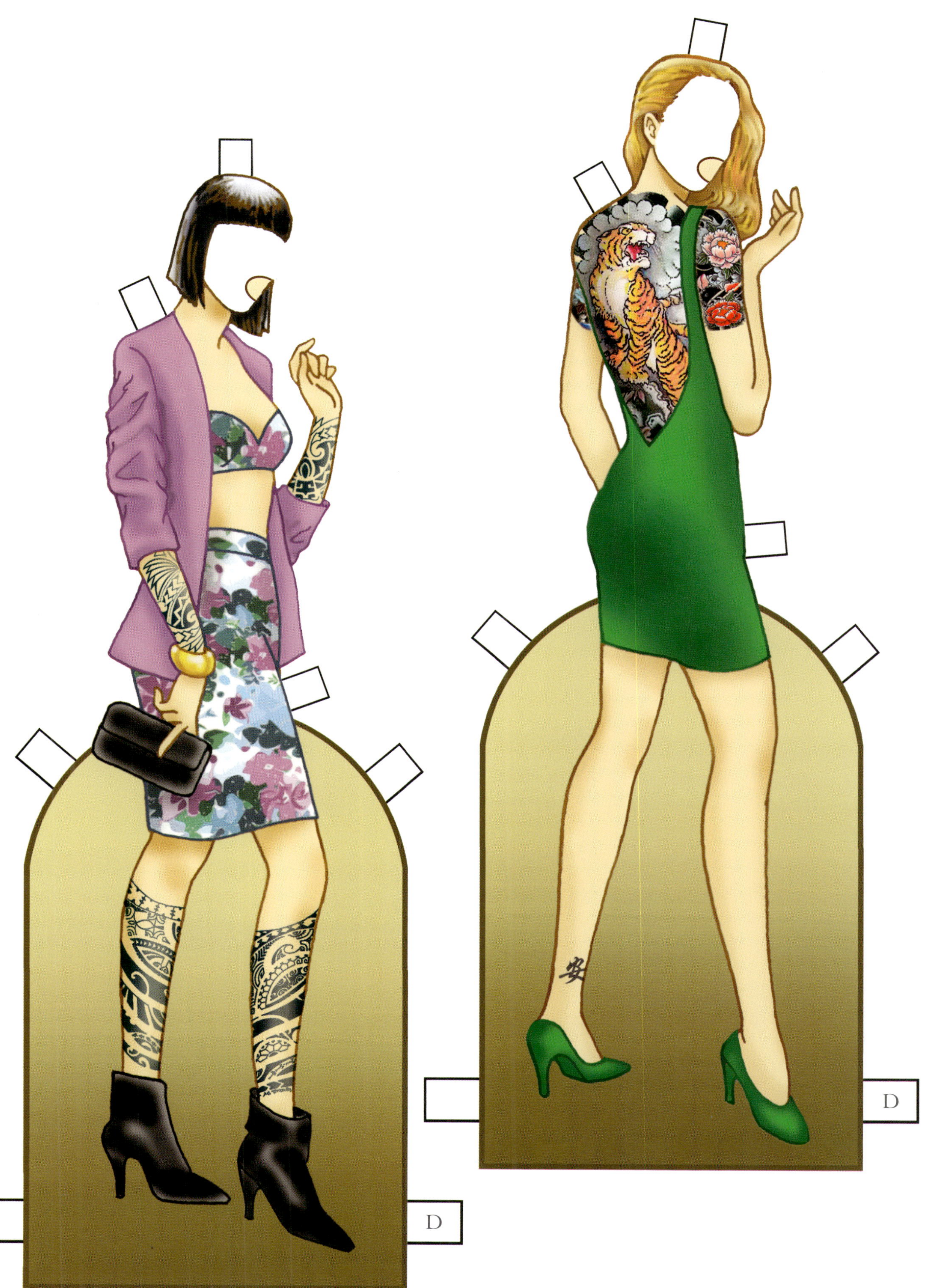
D
D

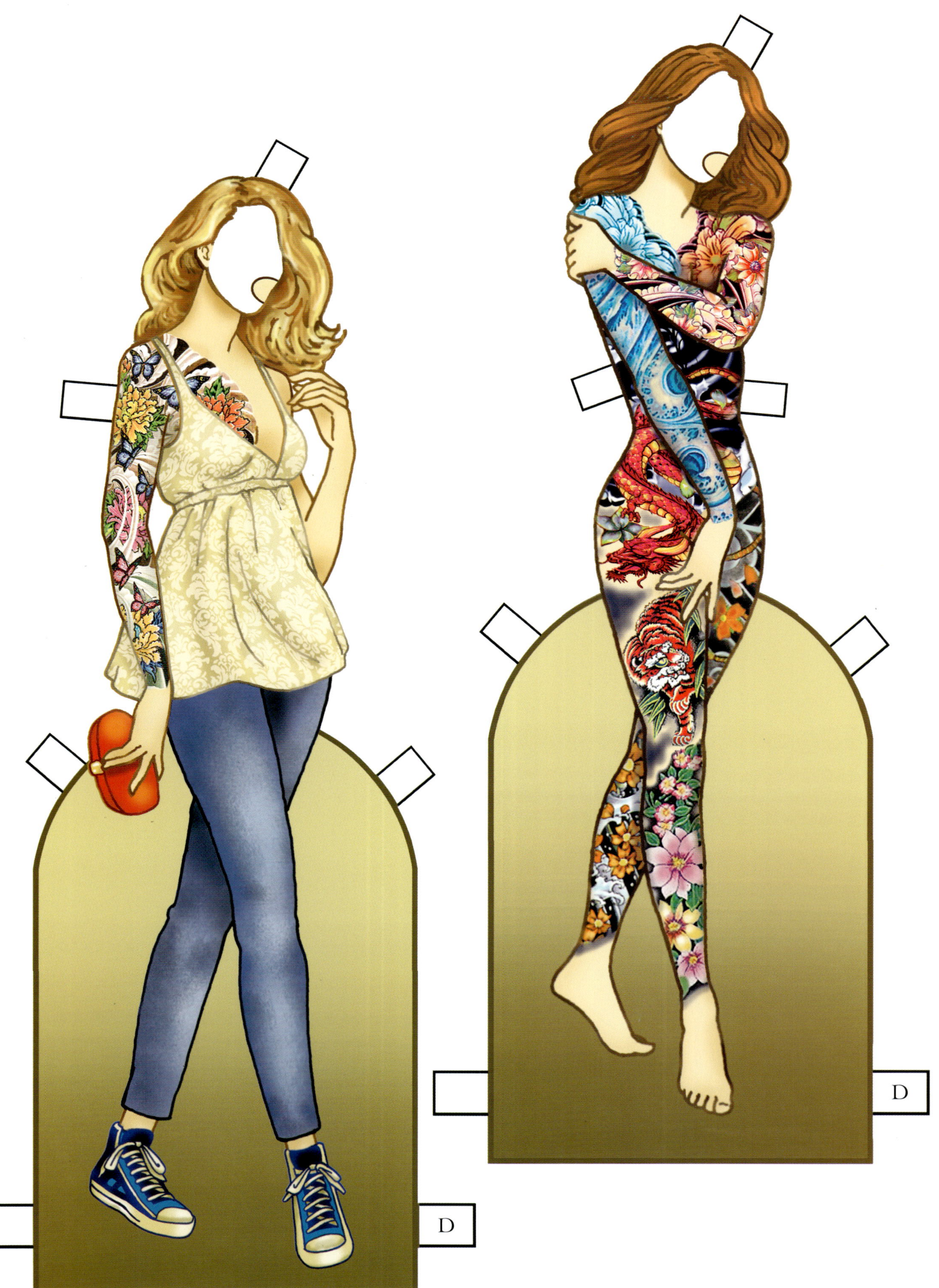
D
D

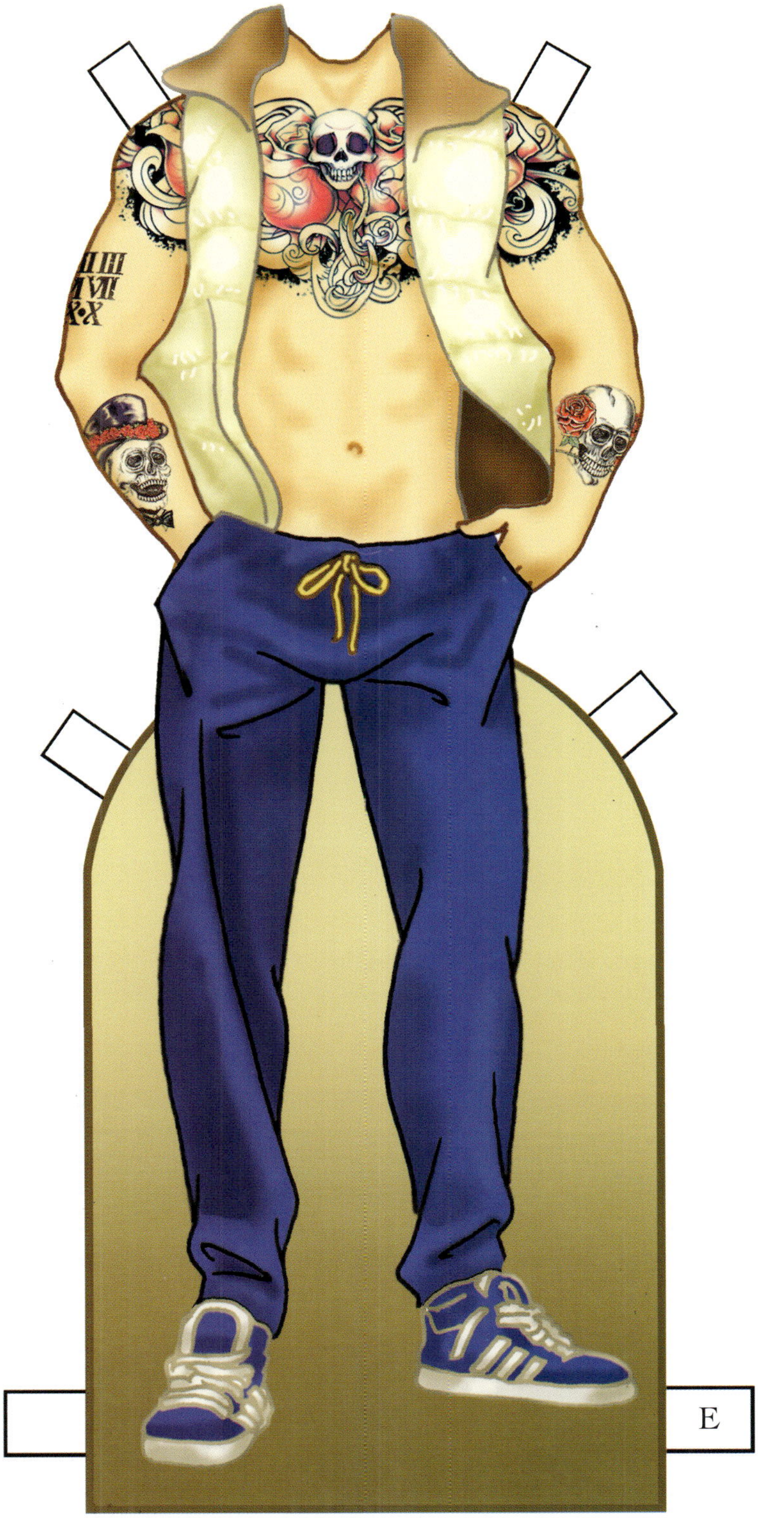

E

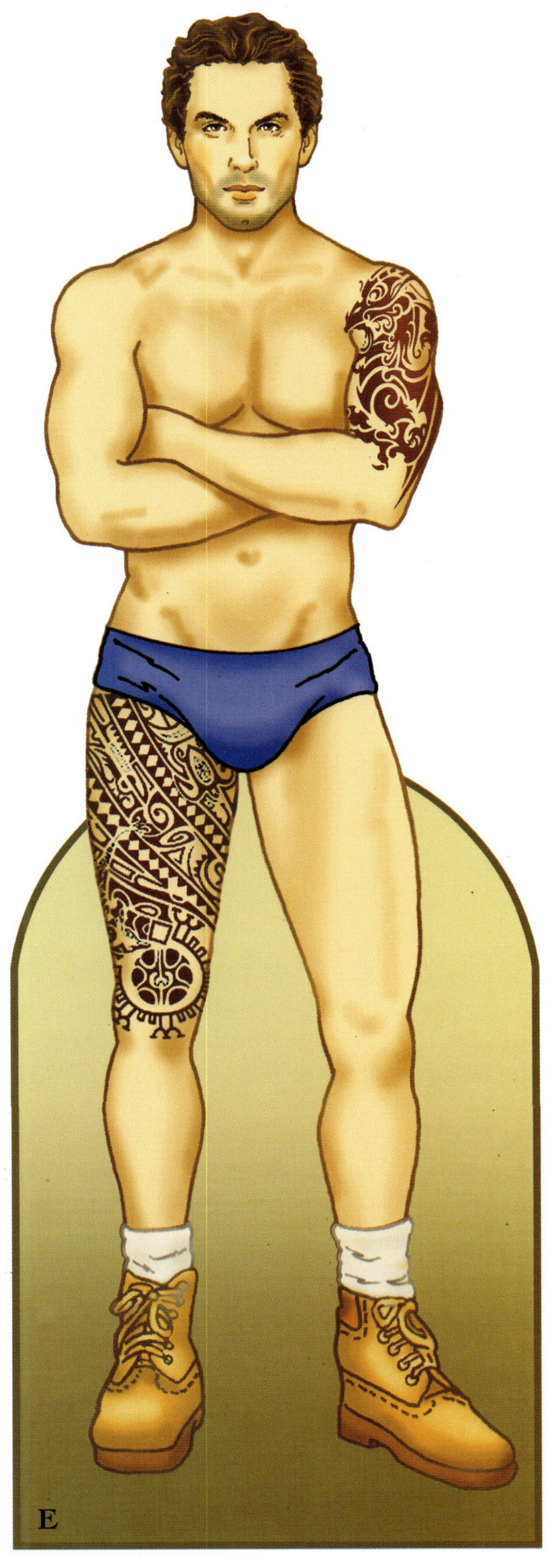

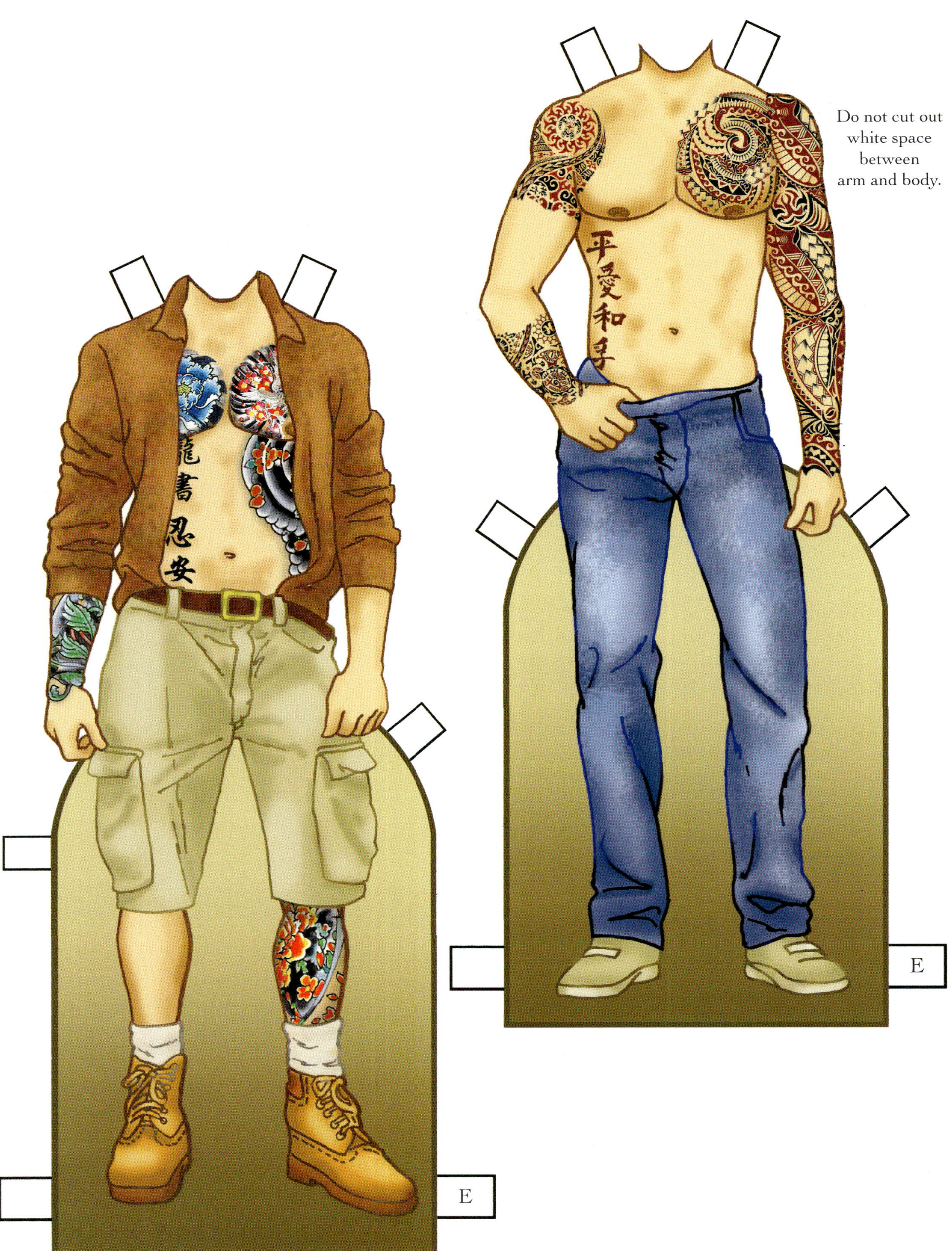

龍書忍安
平愛和手
Do not cut out white space between arm and body.
E
E

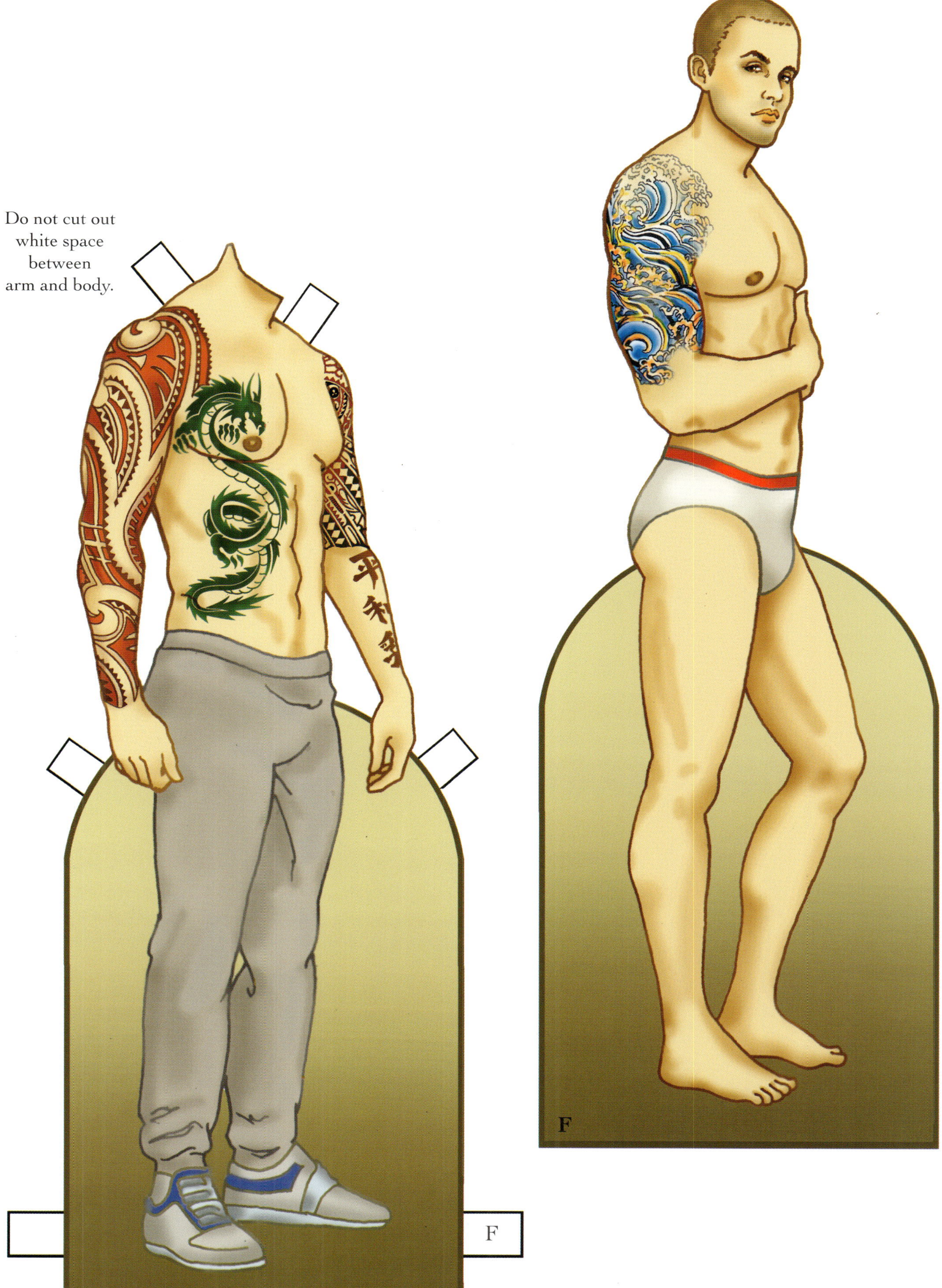
Do not cut out
white space
between
arm and body.
F
F

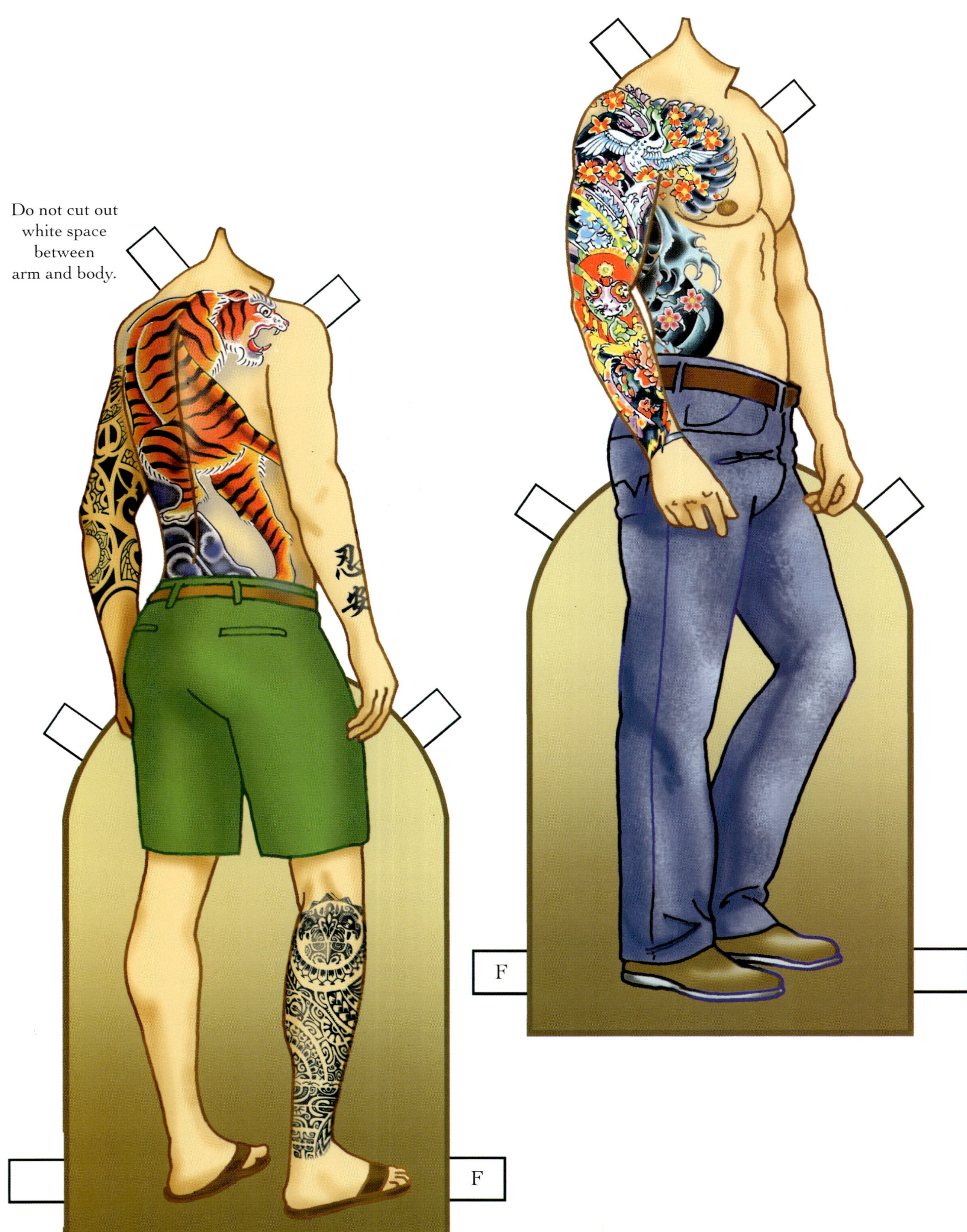
Do not cut out white space between arm and body.
F
F